Build a Compact Garden

BY SAMANTHA S. BELL · ILLUSTRATED BY ROGER STEWART

The Child's World
childsworld.com

Published by The Child's World®
1980 Lookout Drive · Mankato, MN 56003-1705
800-599-READ · www.childsworld.com

Acknowledgments
The Child's World®: Mary Swensen, Publishing Director
Red Line Editorial: Editorial direction and production
The Design Lab: Design

Photographs ©: Life Size Images/iStockphoto, 5; iStockphoto, 6,
8, 9; Wave Break Media/iStockphoto, 7

Design Elements: JosephTodaro/Texturevault; Shutterstock Images

ISBN 9781503807846

LCCN 2015958137

Printed in the United States of America
Mankato, MN
June, 2016
PA02301

ABOUT THE AUTHOR

Samantha S. Bell is the author of more than 30 nonfiction books for children. She loves spending time in her yard in South Carolina, where her family is already busy building a new lasagna garden.

ABOUT THE ILLUSTRATOR

Roger Stewart has been an artist and illustrator for more than 30 years. His first job involved drawing aircraft parts. Since then, he has worked in advertising, design, film, and publishing. Roger has lived in London, England, and Sydney, Australia, but he now lives on the southern coast of England.

Contents

CHAPTER ONE

Small Garden, Big Rewards

When you think about growing vegetables, do you think of a farm? Maybe you think of a big tractor pulling a plow. But did you know you can grow your own garden with just a little bit of space?

A compact garden is a garden in a small area. It could be in a corner of a backyard. It might be on a patio or balcony in a city. Some people even have gardens on their rooftops!

A compact garden can give you fresh food. Fruits and vegetables from a garden are full of **nutrients**. The nutrients help keep you healthy. You can also grow **herbs** in your garden. Cooking with herbs gives food more flavor.

MONEY MATTERS

Growing vegetables is a good way to save money. You will not have to buy them from the store. You can also earn money with a garden. You can sell any extra food you grow.

Gardens are good for us in other ways, too. Taking care of a garden helps people get exercise. You may need to lift, push, pull, or stretch when you are in your garden. Gardening also lets you exercise your brain. You can learn about different plants. Then you can choose which ones to grow. You can be creative with a garden, too. You can make it any size or shape. You can grow many different colorful plants.

Gardening is a good way to relax. Spending time with nature can help you become less stressed or nervous. Gardening is also a good way to enjoy time with family, friends, and neighbors.

In your garden, you can grow vegetables, such as sweet potatoes, for your family to eat.

CHAPTER TWO

Growing Green

Your garden can be good for Earth, too. Some farmers use chemicals to keep insects away. These chemicals also make crops grow bigger or faster. But chemicals can hurt nature. Wind and water can carry them away from gardens. The chemicals can kill plants and animals they were not meant to. You can build a garden without using any chemicals.

When a garden isn't treated with chemicals, it is called an **organic** garden. Organic gardens are good for nature. They allow helpful organisms to live and grow. Bees pollinate the plants.

People often spray chemicals onto their plants.

Ladybugs and ground beetles eat harmful insects. Earthworms create good soil.

Gardens without chemicals are safer for people, too. Chemicals can get into streams and rivers. They can pollute the water supply. Soil is also healthier without chemicals. It holds nutrients and water better. This allows plants to grow stronger.

Organic gardens are also good for the atmosphere. Soil with a lot of nutrients holds more carbon dioxide. This makes it so there is less in the air. Too much carbon dioxide in the air can add to global warming. Global warming can cause storms and big changes in weather.

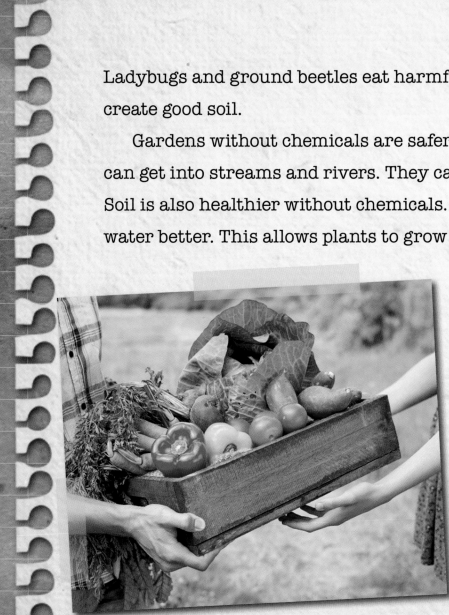

Many people prefer to eat organic food.

CHAPTER THREE

Lasagna Garden

There are many ways to make compact gardens. Some people make container gardens. These gardens grow in pots or barrels.

Raised-bed gardens can sit high above the ground.

People with more space can make raised-bed gardens. These gardens sit on top of the ground. They have small walls around them. Gardeners fill the walled-in spaces with soil. People make square-foot gardens by separating an area into squares. Different plants are planted in each square.

Lasagna gardens are another type of compact garden. They use soil made the natural way. In nature, trees are always losing their branches, twigs, and leaves. Flowers die and fall off. These **decompose** on the ground. Over time, they become rich, dark soil.

Lasagna gardens also use leaves, twigs, and flowers. They use grass **clippings** and vegetable scraps, too. These are placed in layers, like the layers within lasagna. The layers decompose to become rich soil for plants. You do not need to use chemicals on your lasagna garden. The soil is good for the earth. Your compact lasagna garden will look a little messy. But what comes out of the ground will be delicious!

Food scraps can help create good soil for a lasagna garden.

CHAPTER FOUR

Building a Compact Lasagna Garden

MATERIALS

- ☐ Brown materials: fallen leaves, twigs, bark, pine needles
- ☐ Green materials: vegetable scraps, eggshells, coffee grounds, grass clippings, dead flowers, tea bags, peat moss
- ☐ 20 feet (6 m) of rope or string
- ☐ 4 wooden stakes
- ☐ Garden hose
- ☐ Newspaper
- ☐ Shovel
- ☐ Tape measure
- ☐ Potting soil
- ☐ Seeds or seedlings
- ☐ Calendar

There are many ways to build a lasagna garden. It helps to make a plan. Start by finding the best location. The plants in your garden will need a lot of sunlight to grow. Choose a place that gets at least four to six hours of sunlight every day. Your plants will also need water. Make sure a hose can reach the area. Choose a location that is easy to see. You will want to know if there is trouble in your garden. Sometimes insects eat the plants. Other times the plants get diseases. You will also want to watch your plants grow. Let's get started!

INSTRUCTIONS

STEP 1: Collect brown and green materials. Make two separate piles near your garden. Brown materials include dry leaves, twigs, bark, and pine needles. Green materials are fresher. They include grass clippings and vegetable scraps. Eggshells are white, but they count as green material, too. Do not use anything that has meat or oils in it.

STEP 2: Decide how big your garden will be. It's a good idea to start with a small garden. You can make it bigger later. Put a wooden stake at each corner of your garden. Use a string or rope to mark the size and shape of your garden.

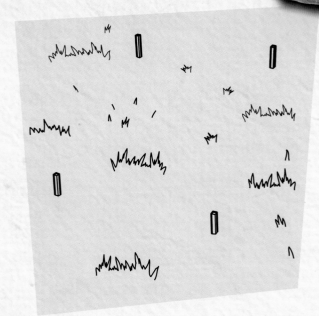

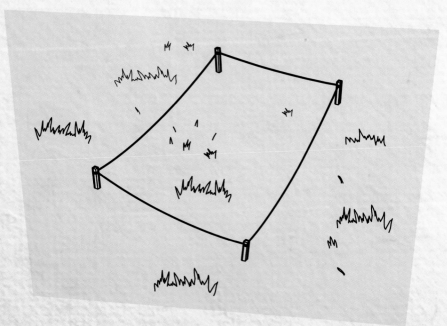

SUNFLOWER HOUSE

You can make walls around your garden with sunflowers. Every 12 inches (30 cm), dig a hole 1 inch (2.5 cm) deep. Put two seeds in each hole. Leave a 2-foot (.6 m) space for a doorway. Watch the flowers grow. Soon you will have a sunflower house!

STEP 3: Pick the kinds of plants you will grow. Vegetables such as onions, carrots, and beets are good to start with. Herbs such as sage and chives are fun to grow, too. Don't forget flowers! They will add a lot of color to your garden.

Flowers also attract birds. Birds eat insects that would harm your garden. **Marigolds** keep harmful insects away, too. You can be creative as you choose your plants. You can make a pizza garden with peppers, tomatoes, and onions. You could plant a salad garden with lettuce, cucumbers, tomatoes, and spinach. Use your imagination. Your garden will be one of a kind!

STEP 4: Cover the garden area with three layers of newspaper. Lay the newspaper on top of the grass. It will break down and create good soil. The newspaper will also help keep weeds from growing in your garden. Overlap the pieces of newspaper to make sure the ground is covered.

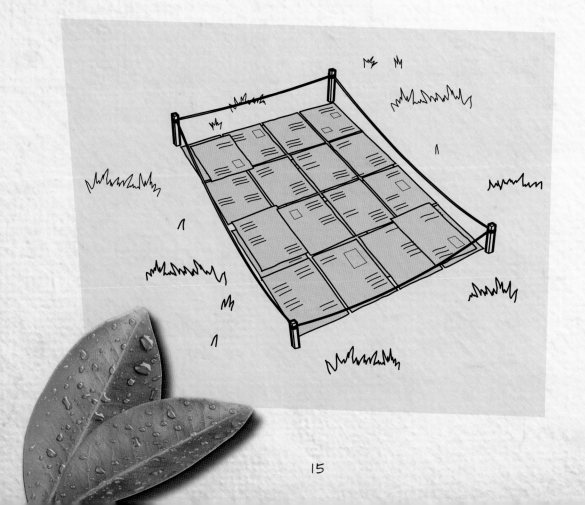

STEP 5: Water the newspaper with the hose. Make sure it is wet. Earthworms like dark, damp areas. They will come to the newspaper. The worms help the layers break down. They also keep the soil loose as they move. Plants grow better in loose soil.

STEP 6: Shovel a layer of green materials on top of the newspaper. Make it about 2 inches (5 cm) thick. Use your tape measure to measure how high it is. Water the layer.

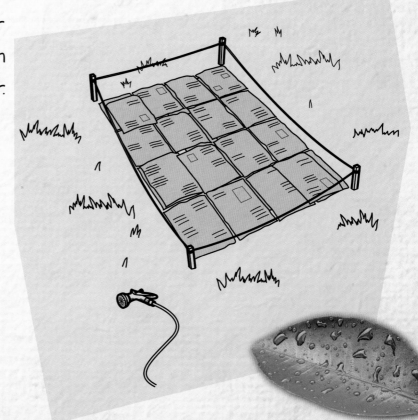

STEP 7: Now add a layer of brown materials. Try to use small pieces. They take less time to break down. Make this layer about 4 inches (10 cm) thick. Water the layer.

STEP 8: Repeat steps 6 and 7 two more times. Make sure to measure and water each layer. When you are done, there should be six layers on top of the newspaper.

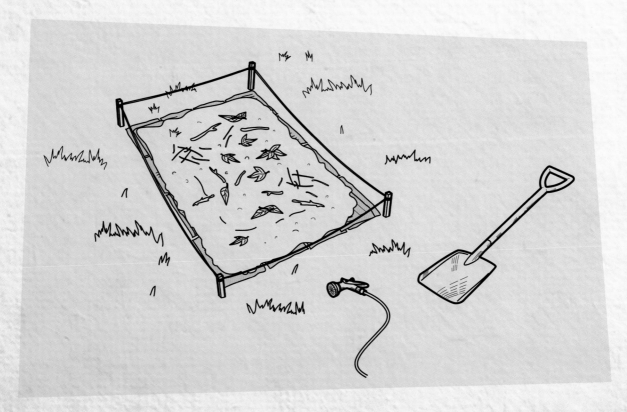

STEP 9: Your garden should be about 18 inches (46 cm) high. You can add more layers of green and brown materials to make it higher. Your garden will not stay this size. As the layers decompose, the garden will shrink. Cover the top layer with **potting soil**.

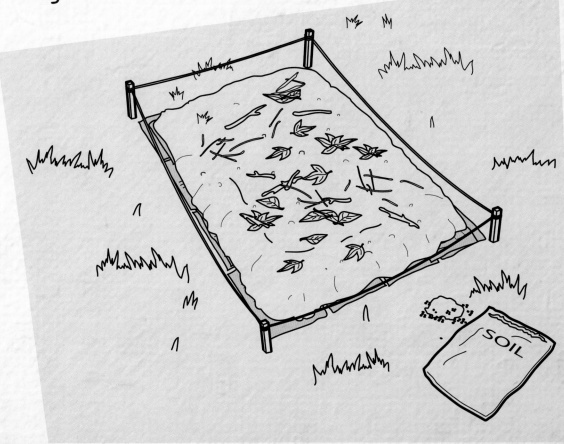

STEP 10: To plant seeds, make a hole in the potting soil. Read the seed package to see how deep to make the hole and how far apart to put the seeds. For **seedlings**, pull the layers apart. Set one plant in each hole. Cover the roots. You can plant in rows but do not need to.

STEP 11: Refill the holes with potting soil.

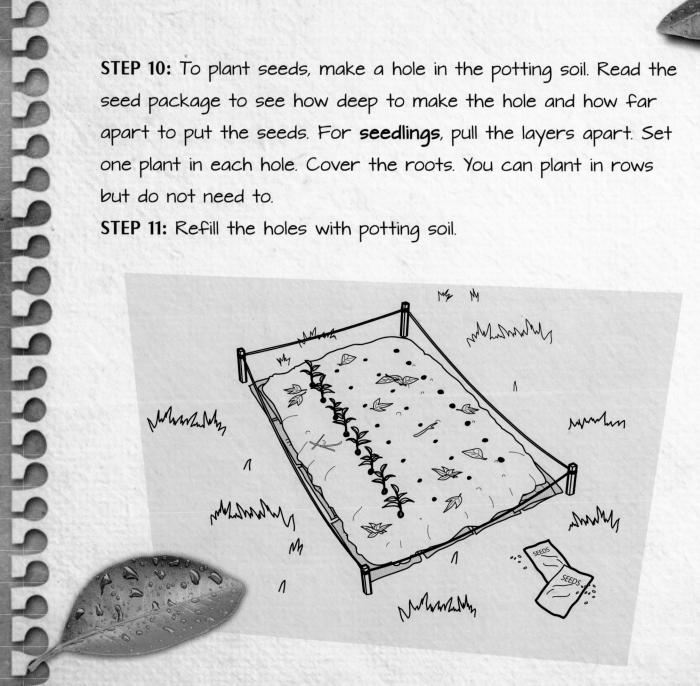

STEP 12: Water your garden when the layers seem dry. The water will help the layers break down.

STEP 13: Keep track of your gardening chores on a calendar. Mark the days you water or check for insects. Some insects help your garden. Others will hurt it. With a parent or teacher, find out how to remove the harmful ones.

STEP 14: Be sure to mark the days you see the vegetables, too. Pick them as soon as they are ripe. Then you can share your vegetables with family and friends!

INSECTS AND YOUR GARDEN

Watch your garden for insects. Some insects will harm your plants. Aphids are tiny green insects that feed on plants. Cutworms are caterpillars that eat plants at night. Slugs are not insects. But they too are pests. They can eat a plant faster than it can grow. Some insects are good for your garden. Ladybugs eat aphids. Ground beetles eat slugs. Spiders also help protect plants. Spiderwebs catch harmful insects.

GLOSSARY

clippings (KLIP-ings) Grass clippings are left behind when a mower cuts a lawn. Grass clippings are green materials that can be added to a garden.

decompose (dee-kuhm-POSE) When something starts to decompose, it breaks down through natural processes. Fallen leaves decompose on the ground.

herbs (URBS) Herbs are plants used for making medicine or seasoning. Herbs are good plants for a new garden.

marigolds (MAR-ri-gohlds) Marigolds are a type of North American flower with gold or red blooms. Marigolds help keep harmful insects out of gardens.

nutrients (NOO-tree-uhnts) Nutrients are substances in food that provide nourishment. Fresh vegetables are full of nutrients.

organic (or-GAN-ik) Foods produced without using artificial chemicals are organic. Organic gardens are good for nature.

potting soil (PAHT-ing soil) Potting soil is a mixture of pine bark, sand, peat, and nutrients. Many people use potting soil for container gardening.

seedlings (SEED-lings) Seedlings are young plants grown from seeds. Some people prefer to plant seedlings.

TO LEARN MORE

In the Library

Gibbons, Gail. *The Vegetables We Eat*. New York: Holiday House, 2008.

Spohn, Rebecca. *Ready, Set, Grow! A Kid's Guide to Gardening*. Tucson, AZ: Good Year, 2007.

Tierra, Lesley. *A Kid's Herb Book: For Children of All Ages*. Bandon, OR: Robert Reed, 2012.

Tornio, Stacy. *Project Garden: A Month-by-Month Guide to Planting, Growing, and Enjoying All Your Backyard Has to Offer*. Avon, MA: Adams Media, 2012.

On the Web

Visit our Web site for links about compact gardens:
childsworld.com/links

Note to Parents, Teachers, and Librarians:
We routinely verify our Web links to make sure
they are safe and active sites. So encourage
your readers to check them out!

INDEX